Adventures in AI: Conversational Journey

Demystifying Artificial Intelligence for Curious Minds

By Akselinc & StackFOSS

Adventures in AI: A Conversational Journey

Demystifying Artificial Intelligence for Curious Minds

Akselinc: Nurturing Open Knowledge

Akselinc is a movement dedicated to nurturing open knowledge and innovation. With a passion for technology and a commitment to accessible education, Akselinc empowers learners and creators worldwide. Through collaborative projects and initiatives, Akselinc envisions a future where knowledge knows no boundaries.

StackFoss: Redefining Learning

StackFoss is a flagship initiative by Akselinc that redefines the way we learn technology. As an open-source powerhouse, StackFoss offers alternatives to mainstream platforms, fostering an environment of collaborative learning. By breaking down barriers and embracing community-driven education, StackFoss empowers individuals to navigate the tech landscape with confidence and creativity.

Content

Introduction: A place at the AI Café

Welcome, dear reader, to our cozy corner of the AI Café, where the aroma of fresh ideas mixes with the intrigue of unexplored territories. Pull up a chair, order your favorite drink, and let's embark on a journey into the world of artificial intelligence, a journey as inviting as a warm conversation with a dear friend.

Now you may be wondering why AI, among other things, captivates us so much. Well, imagine this: a world where machines can learn, adapt, and even make decisions like humans. It's a field where algorithms and data come together to perform tasks that once seemed like science fiction. This is the field of AI, and it is simply fascinating.

You see, the goal of this book is not to inundate you with technical jargon or overwhelm you with complex theories. No, our mission here is to unravel the mystery surrounding AI in a way that is both delightful and enlightening. Together, we'll explore the nooks and crannies of AI, discuss its impact on our lives, and discover the magic that makes it work.

Our promise is simple: it won't be a tedious course or a dry manual. Instead, think of it as a lively conversation with a friend who is just as excited as you are about unlocking the secrets of AI. We'll uncover real-world examples, share stories of AI triumphs and challenges, and most importantly, ensure that you are not just a passive observer but an active participant in this journey.

So, my friend, sip your coffee, settle in, and let's embark on a quest to demystify the enigmatic world of AI: one story, one example, and one conversation at a time.

Chapter 1: A Glimpse into Everyday Lives

In the bustling city of Technoville, where innovation was as common as the morning sunrise, two individuals stood out amidst the crowd. Meet our protagonists: Alex, a dedicated AI enthusiast, and Maya, an endlessly curious novice.

Alex was your typical tech-savvy urbanite. With a perpetually inquisitive glint in his eye and a knack for deciphering complex codes, he navigated the city's digital labyrinth like a seasoned explorer. By day, he was a software engineer, crafting elegant algorithms that powered the future. By night, he delved into the mysterious realms of AI, voraciously consuming every book, article, and online course he could find.

Maya, on the other hand, was a spirited artist with a penchant for colorful canvases and whimsical melodies. She meandered through the city streets, her imagination her constant companion. While technology had always been somewhat of a mystery to her, she possessed an insatiable curiosity about the digital world that surrounded her.

As we peer into their lives, we find Alex meticulously fine-tuning a neural network at his cluttered desk, sipping on coffee as he pondered the next AI breakthrough. Meanwhile, Maya could be found in her cozy art studio, capturing the city's essence on canvas or composing soul-stirring music, blissfully unaware of the AI algorithms orchestrating her playlists.

But little did they know that their worlds were on the brink of a fascinating collision, a convergence of passion and curiosity that would lead them down an exhilarating path into the realm of AI. In the chapters that follow, we'll join Alex and Maya on their everyday adventures, gradually uncovering the enchanting universe of Artificial Intelligence that awaited them just around the corner.

Chapter 2: The Birth of AI: Pioneers and Dreamers

Early on, when the digital age was in its infancy, a group of pioneers and dreamers set out on a journey that would forever change the course of human history. They are the pioneers of artificial intelligence and their stories are nothing short of inspiring.

Alan Turing and the imitation game:

In the midst of World War II, the world was plunged into turmoil. The Allies struggle to decode the secret messages encrypted by the formidable German Enigma machine. It was a time when every piece of information was a matter of life and death.

Amid this chaos, a brilliant mathematician named Alan Turing emerged as an unlikely hero. Turing, with his modest demeanor and mind beyond the bounds of ordinary mortals, was assigned to the codebreaking efforts at Bletchley Park, England.

Turing's genius was undeniable, but it was his bold idea that would change the course of history. You see, Turing was fascinated by the concept of artificial intelligence, the idea that a machine could be designed to think and learn like a human being.

One day, while pondering the intricacies of this concept, Turing conceived what would become known as the "Turing Test." It was a simple but profound proposition: if a machine could engage in a conversation with a human in such a way that the human could not distinguish it from another human, then that machine could be considered intelligent.

Turing's idea was akin to a philosophical paradox, like a riddle designed to challenge the limits of human imagination. But it wasn't just a fanciful idea; it was a visionary concept that laid the foundation for the field of artificial intelligence.

Now imagine Turing, hunched over his desk, surrounded by piles of cryptographic material, working tirelessly to crack the Enigma code. At the time, he was a code breaker extraordinaire, deciphering the enemy's seemingly unbreakable messages. But at night he was a dreamer, imagining a world where machines could think, learn, and solve problems like humans do.

The "imitation game" itself, proposed by Turing as a way to test a machine's intelligence, became the centerpiece of his vision. It was a game of deception, in which a machine's responses during conversation passed for humans or revealed its true mechanical nature. Turing believed that if a machine consistently passed this test, it would be proof of true machine intelligence.

As the war raged, Turing's work was shrouded in secrecy and the brilliance of his ideas was known only to a select few. It was not until decades later that the world fully understood the profound impact of his contributions.

So, my friend, as we sip our coffee and ponder the enigmatic genius of Alan Turing, let us remember that his audacious dream, born in the midst of war, would ultimately light the fires of artificial intelligence, taking us on a journey to across the kingdoms. of machines that think and learn – a journey we continue on today.

John McCarthy and the Dartmouth Workshop:

Let us now turn our attention to another luminary in the history of artificial intelligence: John McCarthy. In the summer of 1956, McCarthy was poised to orchestrate a historic gathering at Dartmouth College that would forever change the trajectory of technology and human ingenuity.

John McCarthy was not just a computer scientist; he was a visionary with a dream: to create machines capable of thinking, reasoning and learning like humans. His ambitions were as vast as the universe of possibilities that AI could open up.

As the sun set on the peaceful campus of Dartmouth College, a group of like-minded pioneers and dreamers converged for an event that will go down in history as the birthplace of artificial intelligence. It was the Dartmouth Artificial Intelligence Workshop.

Picture this: a picturesque university setting, a summer breeze rustling through the trees, and a group of brilliant minds gathered to discuss the seemingly impossible: creating machines that can simulate human intelligence. McCarthy, with his charisma and conviction, led the charge.

The participants were an eclectic mix: mathematicians, computer scientists and even psychologists. They came with a common goal: to explore the uncharted waters of AI. And together they coined the term "Artificial Intelligence" during those fateful weeks in Hanover, New Hampshire.

The vision was bold. They believed that machines, given the proper algorithms and programming, could imitate human thought processes. They imagined machines capable of learning, solving problems and adapting to new challenges. It was a notion that challenged the limits of what was deemed possible in the age of punch card computing.

During the workshop, discussions were lively and ideas flowed like a river. They talked about natural language processing, neural networks (yes, they were already talking about it), problem-solving algorithms, etc. It was as if they were painting the canvas of a new world, one in which machines would become intelligent collaborators.

The Dartmouth workshop sowed the seeds of AI research. This sparked curiosity, collaboration and a shared belief that AI could become a reality. Although they may not have fully grasped the immense challenges ahead, they had taken the first step toward realizing the dream of creating intelligent machines.

As we sit here, telling the story of John McCarthy and the Dartmouth Workshop, we cannot help but marvel at the audacity and vision of these pioneers. They embarked on a journey that would take us into the uncharted territory of artificial intelligence: a journey filled with triumphs, setbacks and a relentless quest for the impossible. And it all started on a sunny summer day in Hannover, where the seeds of AI were sown, waiting to become the technological marvels we see today.

The Chessmaster and the Machine (1950s-1997):

Our narrative takes an exciting twist to the world of chess—a realm where strategy, intellect, and cunning come together in the most captivating of battles. It was in this arena that the aspirations of AI would face one of its most legendary challenges.

The story begins in the 1950s, a time when computers were immense, room-filling beasts with processing power dwarfed by today's smartphones. Yet, the notion of pitting a machine against a human grandmaster had begun to simmer in the minds of AI enthusiasts.

One of these enthusiasts was Alan Turing himself, the visionary we encountered earlier, who had laid the theoretical groundwork for machine intelligence. Turing had foreseen the potential for computers to play chess at a high level, but the technology of his time couldn't quite match his vision.

Fast forward to the 1960s and '70s, and chess-playing programs had started to emerge. They were rudimentary by today's standards, but they kindled a spark of hope in the hearts of AI researchers. Chess, with its well-defined rules and strategic complexity, seemed like the ideal testing ground for machine intelligence.

And then, in the 1970s, a computer program called "Chess 4.0" made waves by becoming the first to defeat a human chess master, David Levy. It was a moment of triumph, albeit on a smaller scale.

But the big moment—the one that would go down in history—was yet to come. It arrived in 1997 when the world chess champion, Garry Kasparov, faced off against IBM's Deep Blue, a computer program that was the pinnacle of AI and computing technology at the time.

The match was nothing short of a global spectacle. The reigning world champion, the embodiment of human chess genius, squared off against a machine that processed an astonishing 200 million positions per second. It was humanity's ultimate chess player pitted against the product of human ingenuity and relentless computation.

The games were tense, the strategies brilliant, and the stakes incredibly high. Deep Blue shocked the world when it won the first game, marking the first time a reigning world champion had lost to a computer under standard chess tournament conditions.

Yet, Kasparov was no ordinary opponent. He came back to win the second game, setting up a nail-biting showdown. In the end, Deep Blue emerged victorious, winning the match by two games to one.

The match was a watershed moment for AI. It demonstrated that computers could surpass human expertise in complex, strategic endeavors. It wasn't just a victory for IBM or AI researchers; it was a triumph for the very idea that machines could mimic and even exceed human intelligence in specific domains.

As we savor this thrilling chapter in the history of AI, we can't help but marvel at the collision of human genius and machine computation. It was a moment when the boundaries of what was thought possible were stretched, and AI was propelled into the realm of practical applications. The Chessmaster and the Machine had left an indelible mark on the landscape of technology and human achievement.

The AI Winter (1970s-1980s):

Our narrative takes a somber turn as we delve into a period known as the "AI Winter." It was a time when the once-burgeoning field of Artificial Intelligence faced chilly headwinds and a relentless freeze in progress.

Picture the world in the 1970s and 1980s—a landscape transformed by the rapid rise of computers and digital technologies. The optimism surrounding AI in the previous decades had been infectious, with promises of intelligent machines that could understand natural language, solve complex problems, and even mimic human reasoning. It was a vision of a future where AI would become an integral part of our lives.

However, as the 1970s dawned, it became apparent that realizing these grand visions was no simple task. The field of AI faced a series of formidable challenges:

1. Limited Computing Power: The computers of the era were still in their infancy, with processing power that paled in comparison to today's devices. AI algorithms, which demanded substantial computational resources, often proved too ambitious for the available technology.

2. High Expectations, Slow Progress: The initial excitement about AI had set expectations sky-high. Many believed that intelligent machines were just around the corner, but the complexity of human cognition proved far more formidable than anticipated. Progress was slow, and early AI systems struggled to perform even basic tasks with any level of reliability.

3. Funding Dwindled: With the gap widening between expectations and reality, funding for AI research began to dry up. Government agencies and private investors, initially enthusiastic about the potential of AI, grew disillusioned as breakthroughs failed to materialize.

It was during this time that the term "AI Winter" was coined—a metaphorical expression of the field's apparent stagnation and loss of momentum. AI research, which had once been bridging with enthusiasm and optimism, now found itself navigating a harsh and icy terrain.

However, let's not forget the resilience of the human spirit, especially when fueled by curiosity and determination. While AI research faced headwinds during the AI Winter, it did not come to a standstill. Researchers continued to explore and develop new algorithms, albeit at a slower pace.

The AI Winter, as challenging as it was, provided valuable lessons. It underscored the importance of managing expectations and aligning them with the capabilities of existing technology. It also highlighted the need for a more pragmatic and incremental approach to AI research.

And so, as we reflect on this chapter in the history of AI, we recognize that it was not a death knell for the field but rather a period of introspection and regrouping. AI was far from defeated; it was merely pausing, gathering strength, and preparing for a resurgence—one that would usher in an era of remarkable progress and innovation.

The resurgence (late 1990s):

Our narrative shifts toward brighter horizons as we delve into the late 1990s, a time when the cold grip of the "AI winter" was beginning to thaw and the seeds of artificial intelligence were about to sprout again.

As the 20th century draws to a close, the world is witnessing a renewed interest in artificial intelligence. The cold winter of AI is slowly giving way to a new dawn of possibilities, and it is during this time that AI is experiencing a resurgence, marked by significant advances and renewed optimism.

Imagine the late 1990s, a period of technological innovation and anticipation of the next millennium. Computers have become more powerful, and the Internet weaves a digital tapestry connecting people and knowledge across the world. It is in this context that AI research has begun to regain momentum.

One of the defining moments of this resurgence was the famous battle on the chessboard, a competition between human intellect and machine calculation. In 1997, world chess champion Garry Kasparov took on IBM's Deep Blue, a computer program with advanced algorithms and computing power.

The match was an epic clash of wits, strategy and calculation. The world watched in awe as Kasparov, the reigning chess champion and symbol of human intelligence, took on an opponent who processed an astonishing 200 million positions per second. Deep Blue won the first match, stunning the world and marking the first time a reigning world champion had lost to a computer under standard tournament conditions.

But Kasparov's spirit was not broken and he came back to win the second game, setting up a dramatic showdown. In the end, Deep Blue emerged victorious, winning the match by two games to one.

It was a moment that reverberated around the world – a testament to the incredible power of AI and computing.

The Deep Blue-Kasparov match has become a symbol of the resurgence of AI. He showed that computers could excel at tasks that required extensive calculations and strategic thinking, pushing the boundaries of human expertise.

But the resurgence of AI has not been limited to the chessboard. AI found applications in diverse fields, from natural language processing to robotics. Search engines like Google used machine learning to improve search results, recommendation systems began to predict our preferences on platforms like Netflix and Amazon, and AI-powered virtual assistants began to respond to our questions and to help us with our tasks.

The end of the 1990s marked the renaissance of AI, a time when researchers, driven by renewed enthusiasm, pushed the limits of what was possible. Lessons learned from AI Winter have led to a more pragmatic and incremental approach, resulting in tangible progress and practical applications.

Reflecting on this resurgence, we see that it wasn't just a return to form for AI; it was a declaration of its enduring potential. The late 1990s ushered in a new era of innovation, one that would propel artificial intelligence into our daily lives and shape the world we know today.

The Deep Learning revolution (2010s to present):

Our story now brings us to the most exciting and transformative chapter in the history of artificial intelligence: the Deep Learning revolution. In the 2010s, a seismic shift occurred that propelled AI into unprecedented areas of success and innovation.

Imagine the world in the early 2010s, a time when digital technologies were deeply ingrained in our daily lives. The seeds of AI, sown over decades of research and development, were about to burst into a forest of possibilities, thanks to an advancement known as deep learning.

Deep learning, inspired by the complex neural networks of the human brain, has marked a paradigm shift in AI research. These deep neural networks, with multiple layers of interconnected artificial neurons, have demonstrated a remarkable ability to understand patterns, recognize objects, and process information in ways that were previously the stuff of science fiction.

One of the most iconic moments of this revolution took place in 2012, when a deep learning model named AlexNet triumphed in the ImageNet competition, beating human performance in object recognition. This victory was a turning point, demonstrating the astonishing capabilities of deep neural networks.

But it wasn't just about image recognition; deep learning has started to shine in various fields:

1. Natural language processing (NLP): Deep learning models such as recurrent neural networks (RNN) and transformers have begun to unlock the mysteries of human language. Machines could now understand and generate text with remarkable fluidity, leading to the birth of chatbots and AI-based translation services.

2. Computer Vision: Convolutional neural networks (CNNs) have become the backbone of computer vision, enabling machines to perceive and interpret visual information with incredible precision. This technology has found applications in facial recognition, autonomous vehicles and medical imaging.

3. Speech recognition: Deep learning models have revolutionized speech recognition, making voice assistants like Siri and Alexa an integral part of our lives. These systems could now understand and respond to voice commands with astonishing accuracy.

4. Health and Science: Deep learning has been instrumental in advancing medical diagnosis, drug discovery, and scientific research. Machines could analyze medical images, predict diseases and even help design new drugs.

The applications of deep learning seemed limitless, transforming industries and redefining the possibilities of what AI could achieve. Autonomous vehicles navigated city streets using deep learning-based algorithms, and recommendation systems personalized our online experiences with astonishing precision.

This era also saw the rise of open source deep learning frameworks like TensorFlow and PyTorch, making this powerful technology accessible to researchers and developers around the world. This has sparked a global community of AI enthusiasts and led to rapid innovation.

Today, we are witnessing a world profoundly shaped by the Deep Learning revolution. AI has become an integral part of our lives, from the devices we use to the way we work, communicate and access information. It has touched every facet of human existence, from healthcare and finance to entertainment and transportation.

The Deep Learning revolution testifies to the incessant search for knowledge and the unlimited potential of human innovation. This has not only transformed AI, but also the way we perceive and interact with the world. And as we look to the future, the possibilities offered by deep learning are as limitless as the human imagination itself.

These pioneers, visionaries and their groundbreaking stories paved the way for the AI-driven world we live in today. Delving into the heart of AI's historical journey, we'll explore the pivotal moments, ethical questions, and incredible achievements that have shaped this remarkable field. So, my friend, let us continue our exploration, guided by the luminous trail left by these early AI pioneers.

Chapter 3: The Building Blocks of AI

Imagine that you are about to embark on a journey to build a magnificent castle. But before you can build towering spiers and sturdy walls, you need a plan, the right materials and skilled craftsmen. Likewise, artificial intelligence, in all its wonders, requires fundamental building blocks to come to life. In this chapter, we'll explore these essential elements: algorithms, data, and machine learning.

Algorithms: The Master Blueprints

Imagine you're building a grand castle from scratch. Before the first stone is laid, you need a detailed blueprint—a set of step-by-step instructions that tell your builders how to create the castle's every nook and cranny. In the realm of Artificial Intelligence (AI), algorithms play the role of these master blueprints.

At their core, algorithms are like recipes for solving problems. Just as a chef follows a recipe to create a delicious meal, AI follows algorithms to perform specific tasks or make decisions. These algorithms are the guiding hand, telling AI what to do, how to do it, and in what order.

Let's make this concept relatable with a familiar example: your GPS navigation system. When you enter a destination and hit "Go," the GPS doesn't just magically know the best route to take. It relies on a complex algorithm that evaluates various paths, calculates distances, and considers real-time traffic data. The algorithm then guides you, turn by turn, to your destination.

In essence, algorithms are the brains behind the operation. They're the reason AI can do amazing things like recognizing your voice, suggesting movies you might like, or even playing chess at a world-champion level.

So, whether it's helping you find the shortest route, recommending your next favorite song, or even diagnosing medical conditions, algorithms are the unsung heroes of AI, quietly shaping the magic that unfolds before your eyes. They are the master blueprints that transform lines of code into intelligent actions.

Data: The Raw Materials

Imagine you're an artisan, crafting a beautiful sculpture. To bring your vision to life, you need the finest materials—clay, marble, or wood. In the world of Artificial Intelligence (AI), data serves as these raw materials, the essential foundation upon which AI constructs its understanding of the world.

Think of data as the treasure find of information that AI relates to to learn, make decisions, and adapt. Just as a sculptor sculpts from raw stone, AI sculpts its intelligence from raw data.

Consider a practical example: your smartphone's virtual assistant. When you ask it a question, like "What's the weather today?" it doesn't have this knowledge stored within like a human. Instead, it accesses a vast database of weather data, which includes historical weather patterns, current conditions, and forecasts. It uses this data to provide you with an accurate answer.

In essence, data is the fuel that powers AI. It comes in various forms, from text and numbers to images and sounds. Every time you browse the internet, post on social media, or use a navigation app, you generate data. Companies and AI systems then collect, process, and analyze this data to improve their services and understand your preferences.

For instance, online shopping platforms like Amazon use your past purchase history and browsing habits to suggest products you might like. This personalized experience is powered by data about your preferences and behavior.

In healthcare, AI can analyze vast datasets of patient records and medical images to help diagnose diseases and recommend treatment options. Data is the bedrock upon which AI's medical knowledge is built.

So, just as a sculptor transforms raw stone into a masterpiece, AI transforms raw data into insights, predictions, and intelligent actions. It's the building block that empowers AI to comprehend the world, adapt to new situations, and provide you with the answers, recommendations, and assistance you need in your daily life. Data is the lifeblood of AI, the precious raw materials that allow it to sculpt intelligence from information.

Machine Learning: The Artisans of Adaptation

Picture this: you have a team of skilled artisans who not only create beautiful sculptures but also improve their craft with each masterpiece they create. This notion of artisans perfecting their skills through experience is at the heart of machine learning—a pivotal component of Artificial Intelligence (AI).

At its core, machine learning is a technology that empowers AI systems to learn, adapt, and improve without being explicitly programmed. It's like having artisans who refine their craft through practice and experience, gradually becoming more skilled and insightful.

Consider a classic example: spam email filters. When you first use a spam filter, it may not catch all the unwanted messages. However, every time you mark an email as spam or not spam, the filter learns from your actions. It recognizes patterns in the emails you receive and refines its ability to distinguish between wanted and unwanted messages. Over time, it becomes remarkably good at keeping your inbox free from spam.

Machine learning is the magic that enables AI systems to recognize patterns, make predictions, and adapt to new information. Just as artisans become better at their craft with each creation, machine learning algorithms become more accurate and efficient as they process more data and learn from their experiences.

In the world of AI, machine learning is the technology behind tasks like:

1. **Speech Recognition:** AI systems that understand and transcribe spoken language improve their accuracy as they encounter more diverse voices and accents.

2. **Computer Vision:** Machines that can recognize objects in images or videos become more proficient with exposure to a wider range of visual data.

3. **Recommendation Systems:** Services like Netflix and Amazon refine their suggestions by learning from your viewing and shopping history.

4. **Language Translation:** AI-powered translation systems get better at converting one language to another through continuous learning from multilingual texts.

Machine learning is what allows AI to become not just smart but also adaptable. It's the reason why your voice assistant understands you better over time, why your email spam filter becomes more effective, and why AI keeps improving in various applications. Just as artisans hone their skills with each creation, machine learning enables AI systems to evolve, making them indispensable in our rapidly changing world.

By combining algorithms, data and machine learning, AI becomes a powerful tool capable of solving complex problems, recognizing faces in photos, translating languages and even playing games like chess and Go to a single player. superhuman level.

As we delve deeper into the world of AI, remember that these building blocks – algorithms, data and machine learning – are the cornerstone of AI's ability to understand, reason and take insights.

decisions. They are the magic behind the scenes, working together to bring AI to life in ways that can amaze us and help us in our daily lives.

Chapter 4: AI in the Real World: Transforming Industries

In this chapter, we will take a fascinating journey into real-world applications of AI, where science fiction meets reality. AI is no longer limited to the realm of imagination; it actively shapes industries, solves complex problems, and makes our lives more convenient and efficient.

Autonomous cars: navigating the future

Imagine a future where you can sit back, relax, and let your car take the wheel, literally. Self-driving cars, once the stuff of science fiction, are now a reality, thanks to remarkable advances in artificial intelligence (AI).

How it works:

Self-driving cars, also known as autonomous vehicles, rely on a complex mix of sensors, cameras, radars and AI algorithms to navigate the road. These AI-driven vehicles constantly perceive their surroundings, make real-time decisions and transport passengers safely from point A to point B.

Advantages:

1. **Safety First:** Self-driving cars have the potential to significantly reduce accidents caused by human error, such as distracted driving or impairment.

2. **Reduced traffic congestion:** Autonomous vehicles can communicate with each other and with traffic systems, thereby optimizing traffic flow and reducing congestion.

3. **Accessibility:** Self-driving cars can provide mobility solutions for people with disabilities, the elderly, and those who cannot drive for various reasons.

Achievements:

1. **Waymo:** An autonomous vehicle subsidiary of Alphabet Inc. (Google's parent company), Waymo was a pioneer in the self-driving car industry. Their vehicles have traveled millions of miles on public roads and are considered one of the most advanced autonomous systems.

2. **Tesla:** Tesla's "Autopilot" feature offers advanced driver assistance capabilities, and they continue to develop fully autonomous driving technology, regularly rolling out updates to improve the performance of the system.

3. **Uber and Lyft:** Ride-sharing companies like Uber and Lyft have invested in autonomous vehicle technology to reduce operating costs and improve safety.

Challenges:

While the promise of self-driving cars is immense, significant challenges remain, including regulatory hurdles, safety concerns and the need for robust AI systems that can handle complex and unpredictable driving scenarios.

Despite these challenges, the future of self-driving cars looks bright. As AI continues to advance, autonomous vehicles could soon become commonplace on our roads, revolutionizing transportation and making our travels safer and more convenient. So buckle up and get ready to let AI guide you into the future of mobility.

Virtual Assistants: Your AI Companions

In the digital age, imagine having a reliable companion always at your disposal, ready to help you with your requests, your tasks and even to brighten your day with a touch of humor. This is the reality of virtual assistants, powered by artificial intelligence (AI). They are not just tools; they are your AI companions in the digital world.

How they work:

Virtual assistants like Siri, Google Assistant and Alexa are the result of cutting-edge AI technologies, including natural language processing (NLP) and machine learning. These AI systems are designed to understand human language, both spoken and written, and respond in a way that resembles natural conversation.

Their abilities:

1. **Answers to Questions:** Virtual assistants can provide answers to a wide range of questions, from trivia and facts to practical information like weather forecasts and sports scores.

2. **Task Automation:** They can set reminders, send messages, schedule appointments, and even control smart home devices, making your life more convenient.

3. **Entertainment:** Virtual assistants can play music, tell jokes and engage in light conversations, adding a touch of fun to your day.

4. **Information Search and Retrieval:** They can search the Internet for you, find nearby restaurants, and provide driving directions, turning your voice into a powerful search tool.

Achievements:

1. **Siri (Apple):** Launched in 2011, Siri was one of the first widely adopted virtual assistants and remains a popular feature on Apple devices.

2. **Google Assistant:** Built into Android devices and available on iOS, Google Assistant is known for its robust search capabilities and in-depth insights.

3. **Amazon Alexa:** Alexa powers Amazon Echo devices, making them a central platform for controlling smart homes and accessing a wide range of services and skills.

Adaptation and learning:

Virtual assistants continually adapt and improve. They learn from your interactions and understand your voice and preferences better over time. This adaptability makes them valuable companions who evolve with you.

Privacy and Security :

The use of virtual assistants raises privacy and security concerns because they often handle personal information. Companies are working diligently to address these concerns by strengthening security measures and providing users with control over their data.

Future possibilities:

The future holds exciting possibilities for virtual assistants, from better natural language understanding to enhanced personalization. They could integrate even more into our daily lives, helping us accomplish tasks we can't yet imagine.

When interacting with your virtual assistant, remember that it's not just a machine; it's your AI companion, there to help you, inform you and sometimes even entertain you. Whether it's answering a quick question or controlling your smart home, these AI companions are designed to make your life easier and more enjoyable in the digital age.

Healthcare: AI as a lifeline

In the world of healthcare, artificial intelligence (AI) is not just a tool; It's a lifesaver. This is revolutionizing the way healthcare professionals diagnose diseases, develop treatment plans and provide care. Let's explore how AI is having a profound impact on the world of medicine.

Diagnosis and detection of diseases:

One of the most important contributions of AI to healthcare is disease detection and diagnosis. AI algorithms can analyze large amounts of medical data, such as patient records, images (X-rays, MRIs, CT scans), and even genetic information, to identify patterns and abnormalities that human eyes might miss .

For example, in radiology, AI-based systems can help radiologists detect abnormalities in medical images, enabling earlier and more accurate diagnoses of diseases such as cancer, fractures and neurological disorders. This early detection can be a game-changer in terms of patient outcomes.

Personalized treatment plans:

AI also helps healthcare professionals create personalized treatment plans. By analyzing a patient's medical history, genetic makeup, and current health status, AI can recommend tailored treatment options. This level of precision medicine reduces the risk of adverse drug reactions and improves the effectiveness of therapies.

Drug Discovery and Development:

The drug discovery process, which traditionally takes years and costs billions of dollars, is being accelerated using AI. Machine learning models can analyze massive datasets to identify potential drug candidates, predict their effectiveness, and even optimize molecular structures. This accelerates the development of new drugs, which could bring potentially life-saving drugs to market more quickly.

Telemedicine and remote monitoring:

AI plays an important role in telemedicine and remote patient monitoring. Virtual health assistants and chatbots can provide instant medical advice and information, reducing the burden on healthcare professionals and making healthcare more accessible.

Additionally, AI-enabled wearable devices can remotely monitor a patient's vital signs and health parameters. These devices can alert healthcare providers to potential problems, enabling early intervention and reducing hospital readmissions.

Challenges and Ethical Considerations:

While AI holds tremendous promise in healthcare, it also presents challenges, including concerns around privacy, data security, and the need for rigorous validation of AI-based medical tools. Ensuring the responsible and ethical use of AI in healthcare is an ongoing priority.

The Future of Healthcare:

As AI continues to advance, the healthcare industry will witness even more transformative changes. AI-based robots can help during surgeries, AI-based chatbots will provide medical assistance 24/7, and AI algorithms will predict outbreaks and outbreaks.

In healthcare, AI is not just a tool; it is a partner that helps save lives and improve the quality of care. This is a testament to the power of technology to augment human capabilities, thereby improving our ability to diagnose, treat and prevent disease. In an increasingly complex healthcare landscape, AI is emerging as a lifeline for patients and an essential tool for healthcare professionals.

Finance: AI in the trading room

Imagine a bustling trading floor where every second counts and fortunes are made or lost in the blink of an eye. In the world of finance, Artificial Intelligence (AI) has become a powerful ally, particularly in the trading room. AI-powered algorithms are transforming the way financial markets operate, making transactions faster, smarter and more efficient.

Algorithmic Trading: The Power of Speed and Accuracy

AI plays a central role in algorithmic trading, a method that relies on high-speed computer algorithms to make trading decisions. These algorithms can analyze large amounts of financial data, news and market indicators in real time, making split-second decisions to buy or sell assets such as stocks, bonds and securities. currencies.

Key Benefits:

1. **Speed:** AI algorithms execute trades at lightning speed, far surpassing human capabilities. In high-frequency trading (HFT), AI systems can buy and sell assets in fractions of a second, taking advantage of price fluctuations in microseconds.

2. **Data Processing:** AI can process large data sets, including market prices, news sentiment, and economic indicators, to identify business opportunities and risks.

3. **Risk Management:** AI algorithms can automatically manage risks by setting stop-loss limits, diversifying portfolios, and adjusting strategies in response to market conditions.

Quantitative trading: predictive analysis at play

Quantitative traders use AI and machine learning to create predictive models that predict market movements. These models analyze historical data, market trends, and external factors to make informed business decisions.

Key Applications:

1. **Predictive Analysis:** AI models can predict market trends, asset price movements, and economic events, allowing traders to position themselves accordingly.

2. **Portfolio Optimization:** AI algorithms optimize investment portfolios to maximize returns while managing risks.

3. **Risk Assessment:** AI-based risk models assess the potential impact of market events and guide risk management strategies.

Fraud detection and risk assessment: safeguarding the financial ecosystem

AI also plays a key role in safeguarding the financial ecosystem. Machine learning models can detect fraudulent transactions, assess credit risks, and monitor market anomalies in real time.

Key Features:

1. **Fraud Detection:** AI algorithms analyze transaction data to identify unusual patterns or behaviors that may indicate fraud, protecting financial institutions and consumers.

2. **Credit Score:** AI-powered credit scoring models assess borrowers' creditworthiness, streamlining the lending process and reducing the risk of default.

Challenges and Ethical Considerations:

The role of AI in finance raises important ethical considerations, including algorithmic bias, risks of market manipulation and data privacy concerns. Regulators are actively addressing these challenges to ensure responsible use of AI in financial markets.

As AI continues to advance, it will remain a powerful tool on the trading floor, enabling financial institutions to trade more efficiently, effectively manage risk, and make data-driven investment decisions. AI's ability to process large amounts of data and adapt to changing market conditions positions it as an indispensable player in the dynamic world of finance.

Manufacturing: Precision and Efficiency with AI

Imagine a manufacturing plant where every operation is performed with precision, efficiency and minimal errors. This vision has become reality thanks to the integration of artificial intelligence (AI) into the manufacturing process. Let's explore how AI is revolutionizing the manufacturing industry, making it smarter and more efficient than ever.

1. Robotics and automation:

AI-driven robots have transformed manufacturing lines, performing tasks with precision and consistency. These robots can assemble products, perform quality checks and even handle materials that can be dangerous to humans. Their ability to work 24/7 without fatigue increases production capacity and efficiency.

For example, in the automotive industry, robots equipped with computer vision systems can identify defects in car bodies with remarkable accuracy, ensuring that only impeccable vehicles leave the factory.

2. Predictive maintenance:

Downtime in manufacturing can be costly. AI-based predictive maintenance systems use sensors and data analytics to predict when equipment is likely to fail. This proactive approach allows manufacturers to perform maintenance only when necessary, reducing downtime and maintenance costs.

3. Quality control:

AI has raised the bar for quality control. Machine learning models can detect even the smallest product defects, ensuring that only high-quality items reach consumers. This level of precision reduces waste and improves customer satisfaction.

4. Supply Chain Optimization:

AI optimizes the supply chain by forecasting demand, streamlining logistics and managing inventory more efficiently. This not only reduces costs but also ensures that products are available when and where they are needed.

5. Customization and Personalization:

AI-driven manufacturing enables greater product customization. For example, in the fashion industry, AI can help design personalized clothing based on individual preferences and measurements.

6. Energetic efficiency :

Manufacturers are using AI to optimize energy consumption, reducing environmental impact and operating costs. AI algorithms can analyze energy consumption patterns and make real-time adjustments to minimize waste.

7. Research and development:

During product development, AI can simulate and test various design options, leading to more innovative and efficient products. This accelerates the innovation cycle and reduces time to market.

Challenges and Considerations:

While AI offers enormous benefits in the manufacturing sector, it also presents challenges related to data security, privacy and the need for skilled workers to operate and maintain AI-driven systems. Ethical concerns, such as the impact on employment, must also be considered.

The Future of Manufacturing:

As AI continues to evolve, the future of manufacturing looks bright. Smart factories equipped with AI-based systems will operate with greater precision, efficiency and adaptability. Manufacturers will harness the power of data to make real-time decisions, optimize processes and deliver products that meet exacting consumer standards.

In manufacturing, AI is not just a tool; it is a catalyst for transformation. This is shaping the factories of the future, where precision, efficiency and sustainability are the cornerstones of success. With AI as your manufacturing partner, the possibilities are limitless.

Entertainment and Content Creation: AI as an Artist

Imagine a world where AI is not just a tool for creators but a collaborator, an artist in its own right. This is the exciting reality in entertainment and content creation. Artificial intelligence (AI) not only helps artists but also generates captivating and inspiring artwork, music and stories. Let's explore how AI is reshaping the creative landscape.

AI-generated art:

AI algorithms, especially those based on Generative Adversarial Networks (GAN), can produce stunning works of art. These algorithms can analyze large art databases and generate original works in different styles, from classical to abstract. Some AI-generated artworks have even been sold at auction for significant sums.

Musical composition:

AI composes music that touches the heart. Machine learning models can analyze large sets of musical data and generate original compositions. Composers and musicians use AI-generated pieces as inspiration or even as components of their compositions. AI has expanded the possibilities for musical creativity.

Video game development:

AI is a game changer in video game development. AI algorithms can create dynamic, adaptive and unpredictable game worlds. Characters and opponents in games can now learn and react to player actions, making the game more engaging and challenging.

Custom Content:

AI-based recommendation systems, like those used by Netflix and Spotify, tailor content recommendations to individual preferences. These systems analyze your viewing or listening history to suggest movies, shows or songs you might enjoy. This personalization improves user experience and engagement.

Content Improvement:

AI can improve the quality of content. For example, machine learning models can improve video resolution, clean up audio recordings, and even colorize old black-and-white movies. This technology revitalizes classic content and brings it to modern audiences.

Nature :

AI can create compelling stories. Some AI models are capable of generating written narratives, whether news articles, short stories, or even poetry. Even if they do not replace human authors, AI-generated stories offer avenues for creativity and inspiration.

Challenges and Considerations:

AI in entertainment and content creation raises questions about copyright, creativity and the role of the artist. Ethical concerns, such as deepfake technology, also need to be carefully considered.

The future of creativity:

As AI continues to evolve, it will become more and more an integral part of the creative process. Artists will collaborate with AI to push the boundaries of imagination, and AI will become a source of inspiration in its own right.

In entertainment and content creation, AI is not just a tool; it is a co-creator, an amplifier of human creativity and a source of infinite possibilities. It challenges us to redefine what it means to be an artist and invites us to explore uncharted areas of creativity and innovation. With AI as the artist, the entertainment world is poised for an exciting and imaginative future.

These real-world applications are just a glimpse of the transformative power of AI. It reshapes industries, improves our daily lives and opens new frontiers of possibilities. As we explore these remarkable stories, we will witness the impact of AI across diverse industries, from transportation and healthcare to finance and entertainment, and appreciate how it is revolutionizing the way we work, live and interact with the world around us.

Chapter 5: Behind the Curtain: How AI Works

In this chapter, we'll embark on a journey into the inner workings of artificial intelligence (AI), revealing the mysteries of neural networks, deep learning, and AI model training. Using metaphors and analogies, we will shed light on these complex technical concepts to make them more accessible and understandable.

Neural networks: the architects of AI

Imagine that artificial intelligence (AI) is like a great symphony, and that at its heart are the architects of this musical masterpiece: neural networks. These complex structures are designed to mimic the way our brains process information, allowing AI to make sense of the world in a remarkably intelligent way.

Analogy: Think of a neural network as a large network of pipes, each representing a neuron. These pipes are interconnected, forming a complex data flow system. Just as neurons in the brain transmit and process information, these neural network channels transmit and process data. Each channel, or neuron, can make decisions as data passes through it.

In this analogy, imagine that each neuron in the network is responsible for recognizing a specific aspect of the data it encounters, much like individual musicians in an orchestra playing their unique instruments. Together, these neurons create a symphony of information processing, allowing the AI to perform tasks, make decisions and learn from its experiences.

Much like a composer creating a symphony by arranging different instruments and melodies, AI developers design neural networks to perform specific tasks. These networks are made up of layers of interconnected neurons, and the arrangement and connections between these layers determine the network's ability to process information.

As you delve deeper into the world of AI, you'll discover how these neural networks form the foundation upon which AI intelligence is built. These are not simple pipes; it's the composers, conductors, and musicians who bring AI to life, making it capable of recognizing patterns, understanding language, and even playing games with human skills.

Deep Learning: peeling back the layers of intelligence

Think of deep learning as an intriguing process of peeling back the layers of an onion, revealing its fundamental essence. In the field of artificial intelligence (AI), deep learning consists of stacking several layers of computing units within a neural network. These layers work together to process data in increasingly sophisticated and nuanced ways.

Analogy: Think of deep learning like editing a photograph. You start with a base image, then apply a series of filters, each sharpening detail and clarity. As you apply more filters, the image will gradually become sharper and more defined.

In the world of deep learning, these layers of computation serve a similar purpose. Each layer extracts specific features or patterns from the input data, creating a hierarchical representation. Much like peeling the layers of an onion, each layer adds complexity and depth to understanding the data.

For example, in image recognition, the first layer can identify basic edges and shapes, while deeper layers recognize more complex features such as textures or specific objects. Each layer builds on the information extracted by the previous layer, gradually revealing the intricacies of the data.

This hierarchy of layers allows deep learning models to understand data at different levels of abstraction. It's like peeling back the layers of a story: as you dig deeper, you gain a richer, more nuanced understanding of the narrative. Similarly, in deep learning, as you progress through the layers, the AI gains a deeper, more nuanced understanding of the data it encounters.

This concept of peeling back the layers in deep learning is key to AI's ability to understand complex patterns, from recognizing objects in images to understanding the meaning of language. It's like gradually revealing the details of a captivating painting, one layer at a time, until the complete masterpiece is revealed.

Training Models: Nurturing Intelligence

Training AI models is a bit like nurturing intelligence in a growing mind. Just like a child learns from experiences and adjusts their behavior, AI models start from scratch and learn by being exposed to large amounts of data. They gradually refine their understanding and decision-making processes through this exposure.

Analogy: Think of training AI models like teaching tricks to a pet. When you teach a dog to fetch a ball, he doesn't get it right the first time. He learns by trial and error, adjusting his actions based on feedback. Similarly, AI models start from basic knowledge and improve by continually refining their responses.

Here's how the process works:

1. **Start with a clean slate:** AI models start with little or no knowledge about the specific task they are designed to do. They are like a new puppy who doesn't know any tricks yet.

2. **Exposure to Data:** Just like you teach a dog by showing it how to fetch, AI models learn from data. They are exposed to large data sets relevant to their task. For example, a language translation model can be exposed to multilingual texts, while a facial recognition model learns from thousands of images of faces.

3. **Parameter adjustment:** As the model processes this data, it adjusts its internal parameters. Think of these metrics as the dog's muscle memory for reporting: the more he practices, the better he gets. In AI, the model refines these parameters to make more accurate predictions or decisions.

4. **Iterative Learning:** Training is an iterative process. The model examines the data repeatedly, compares its predictions to the correct answers, and refines its parameters. This is similar to how a dog learns by repeating tricks until it succeeds.

5. **Continuous Improvement:** With each iteration, the AI model gets better at its task. It's like watching a pet become more adept at retrieving the ball with each training session. AI models continue to learn and improve as they are exposed to more data and experiences.

So, training AI models is not a one-time event; it is a continuous process of development and improvement. Over time, these models become more and more effective, whether it's language translation, recognizing patterns in images, or making predictions in various domains.

Much like raising an intelligent, adaptable pet, training AI models involves patience, repetition, and providing the right experiences. The result is a well-trained AI capable of performing complex tasks with remarkable precision and efficiency.

Optimization: Fine-Tuning the Orchestra

Imagine that Artificial Intelligence (AI) is like conducting an orchestra, and optimization is the process of fine-tuning each instrument to achieve perfect harmony. In the world of AI, optimization is the critical step that tweaks the parameters of AI models to enhance their performance and accuracy.

Analogy: Think of optimization as a conductor leading an orchestra. The conductor's role is to ensure that each musician and instrument is perfectly synchronized, playing at the right tempo, and hitting the correct notes. In a similar way, optimization ensures that the parameters of AI models are adjusted precisely to achieve the desired outcomes.

Here's how optimization works:

1. **Starting Point:** Just as an orchestra starts with musicians and instruments in their initial state, AI models begin with initial parameter values. These parameters control how the model makes decisions and predictions.

2. **Iterative Refinement:** Optimization is an iterative process, much like rehearsing for a concert. During each iteration, the model's performance is evaluated by comparing its predictions to the desired outcomes (the sheet music). If there are discrepancies, adjustments are made.

3. **Adjusting Parameters:** Optimization involves fine-tuning the model's internal parameters to minimize errors. It's like a conductor giving feedback to musicians, helping them improve their timing and precision. In AI, this fine-tuning helps the model make more accurate predictions or decisions.

4. **Convergence:** Over multiple iterations, the model's parameters gradually converge to optimal values, much like a conductor and orchestra working together to refine their

performance. The model becomes more precise in its tasks as it fine-tunes its parameters.

5. **Performance Improvement:** The ultimate goal of optimization is to improve the model's performance, making it more accurate and efficient. This is similar to an orchestra's performance getting better and better with each rehearsal.

In the world of AI, optimization ensures that AI models perform at their best, whether it's recognizing objects in images, translating languages, or making financial predictions. It's like conducting a symphony where every instrument plays in perfect harmony, creating a beautiful and accurate rendition of the desired outcome.

Just as a conductor's guidance and expertise elevate an orchestra's performance, optimization is the guiding force that refines AI models, making them more capable and accurate with each iteration.

Deep Learning Layers: Unveiling the Complexity

Think of deep learning layers as chapters in a compelling book, each adding depth and complexity to the story. In the world of artificial intelligence (AI), deep learning involves stacking multiple layers of interconnected nodes within a neural network. Just like flipping through the chapters of a book, each layer reveals increasingly complex details, allowing AI to understand data at different levels of abstraction.

Analogy: Think of deep learning layers as chapters in a book. When you start reading a book, you start with the first chapter, which sets the stage and introduces the basic concepts. As you delve deeper into the book, each subsequent chapter adds more complexity and nuance to the story, providing a deeper understanding of the narrative.

In the context of deep learning:

1. **The first layer:** This is like the first chapter of the book, where the most basic features or patterns are identified in the data. It's similar to recognizing simple shapes or edges in an image.

2. **Next Layers:** As you progress through the chapters of a book, deeper layers of the neural network discover more and more complex features. These layers can recognize textures, parts of objects, or specific objects in an image.

3. **The final layers:** These are like the climactic chapters of the book, where the most intricate details and nuances are revealed. In deep learning, the final layers of the network include high-level features, such as recognizing a specific face or object.

By peeling back the layers of the neural network, AI gains a richer, more nuanced understanding of the data it encounters. This hierarchical representation allows it to understand complex patterns, recognize objects in images, understand language, and make predictions with a level of sophistication once thought to be the exclusive domain of human intelligence.

Much like reading a book, where each chapter builds on the previous ones, layers of deep learning allow AI to discover the intricacies of the data step by step. It is a journey of discovery, where the complexity of the world is revealed layer by layer, enriching the understanding and capabilities of AI.

Loss function: Striving for perfection

In the world of artificial intelligence (AI), the loss function serves as a relentless coach critiquing a gymnast's routine, pushing them to strive for perfection. This essential component evaluates how well an AI model's predictions align with actual results, guiding the model to improve with each iteration.

Analogy: Imagine an AI model as a gymnast performing a routine. The goal is to perform flawlessly, but with each attempt there may be minor imperfections. The loss function is like the panel of judges who evaluate the routine and assign a score. The lower the score, the better the performance.

Here's how the process works:

1. **The Gymnast's Routine:** The AI model makes predictions based on the data it encounters, much like a gymnast performs a routine.

2. **Performance Evaluation:** The loss function evaluates the performance of the model by comparing its predictions to the actual results. This assessment identifies gaps between what the model predicted and what actually happened.

3. **Assigning a score:** Just as judges assign scores to a gymnast's routine, the loss function calculates a score that reflects the "loss" or error in the model's predictions. This score quantifies the performance of the model.

4. **Iterative Improvement:** Like a dedicated gymnast who uses feedback from judges to improve their routine, the AI model uses feedback from the loss function to adjust its internal parameters.

These adjustments aim to minimize the loss, which equates to the gymnast aiming for a higher score.

5. **Continuous Refinement:** The AI model repeats this process iteratively, gradually reducing its losses and improving its performance. It's as if the gymnast is practicing their routine over and over to achieve perfection.

The ultimate goal of the loss function is to guide the AI model towards more accurate predictions or decisions. Much like a gymnast's pursuit of a perfect routine, the AI model strives for perfection in its task, continually refining its performance while minimizing losses.

By using the loss function as a coach and evaluator, AI models are able to learn and improve with each iteration, ensuring that they become increasingly accurate and proficient at their respective tasks.

By using these metaphors and analogies, we have pulled back the curtain on the complex mechanics of AI, making neural networks, deep learning and model training more understandable. Like a conductor refining his performance or a pet learning new tricks, AI is a symphony of algorithms and data, continually improving its intelligence with every note and step .

Chapter 6: Challenges and Ethical Dilemmas

In our journey through the realm of Artificial Intelligence (AI), we've discovered its wonders and capabilities. But like any powerful tool, AI brings with it a set of ethical considerations and challenges. Imagine you're sitting with a friend, and you start discussing these intriguing dilemmas surrounding AI.

AI and Bias: The Unseen Prejudice

You explain to your friend how AI systems can unwittingly perpetuate bias. "Imagine," you say, "you're teaching a child to identify fruits, but your teaching materials only include apples and bananas. When the child sees an orange, they might think it's an oddly shaped apple!"

Similarly, AI learns from the data it's given. If that data contains biases, the AI can inherit them. For instance, if a hiring AI is trained on historical data with gender bias, it might unfairly favor one gender over another. This bias can extend to lending decisions, predictive policing, and even healthcare recommendations.

"But," you add, "the good news is that people are working to address this. They're collecting more diverse data, creating tools to detect bias, and establishing ethical guidelines to ensure AI developers are aware of the issue."

AI and Privacy: The Delicate Balance

Shifting the conversation to privacy, you explain, "Imagine having a personal assistant that knows everything about you, even the things you'd rather keep to yourself. It's like living in a glass house where your every move is visible."

AI, with its data-hungry appetite, can raise concerns about personal privacy. It can track our online habits, analyze our conversations, and even recognize our faces in public spaces. This convenience can clash with our need for privacy.

"You see," you say, "it's a delicate balance. We enjoy the convenience AI brings, but we must protect our privacy. That's why there are discussions about data anonymization, encryption, and the need for clear rules to safeguard our personal information ."

AI and Job Displacement: The Changing Landscape

As you sip your coffee, you mention, "Imagine a world where machines do most of the jobs, and humans have to find new roles. It's like a technological revolution reshaping the employment landscape."

AI's automation capabilities raise questions about job displacement. Some fear that AI and robots will replace human workers in various industries. "But," you reassure your friend, "many believe AI will also create new job opportunities. We just need to adapt and learn new skills."

AI and Ethical Decision-Making: Who's Responsible?

"Imagine," you say, "you're in a self-driving car, and it faces an ethical dilemma. Should it protect you at all costs, or should it prioritize the safety of pedestrians, even if it means harming you? Who should make these life-and-death decisions?"

Ethical dilemmas in AI decision-making are real. Developers, companies, and regulators share the responsibility to ensure AI systems make ethical choices. You discuss the challenges of creating ethical AI standards and guidelines, highlighting the need for accountability.

AI and Transparency: Shedding Light on Decisions

"Imagine if AI made decisions, but you had no idea how or why," you suggest. "It's like a magician performing tricks without revealing the secrets behind the illusions."

AI's decisions can be mysterious, making it difficult to understand and trust. Transparency is crucial, and you discuss how AI systems are becoming more transparent, allowing users to understand their decision-making processes.

The Future of AI Ethics: A Call to Action

As you wrap up your conversation with your friend, you emphasize the importance of critical thinking about AI ethics. "We're shaping the future of AI," you say, "and it's our responsibility to ensure it aligns with our values of fairness, privacy, and accountability."

With different viewpoints and open discussions, we can navigate the ethical challenges AI presents. By encouraging critical thinking, we can collectively work towards a future where AI enhances our lives while respecting our ethical principles.

Chapter 7: AI and Creativity

As we delve deeper into the world of artificial intelligence (AI), we discover that it's not just about crunching numbers and solving problems. AI is also an enabler of creativity, revolutionizing creative fields like art and music. Imagine sitting with a friend and sharing stories of AI-generated masterpieces and innovations that are reshaping the creativity landscape.

AI in art: the collaborative muse

Imagine a world where artists have a muse who is not limited by human limitations, a muse who draws inspiration from the entire tapestry of art history and can generate breathtaking new works of art. breath. In the field of artificial intelligence (AI), this is becoming a reality.

Imagine a scenario where artists team up with AI algorithms to create stunning pieces that challenge our perception of creativity. It's not about replacing human artists; it's about expanding their capabilities and pushing the boundaries of imagination.

AI-Generated Masterpiece Stories

Imagine hearing stories of artists who have adopted AI as their collaborative muse. They feed AI systems with centuries of art history, from the Renaissance to 20th-century abstract expressionism.

These artists then set parameters and let AI algorithms generate unique pieces, often in a fusion of styles that no human artist could have imagined. Paintings that blend the techniques of Van Gogh and Picasso with a touch of futuristic abstraction come to life on canvases, leaving art critics and enthusiasts in awe.

Explore unexplored territories

The beauty of AI in art is that it takes artists on journeys through unexplored territories of creativity. They collaborate with algorithms that analyze their existing works, identify their unique style and suggest new directions.

Imagine an artist known for his landscapes partnering with AI to create surreal cityscapes that defy reality or a sculptor working with AI to design complex patterns that seem to defy the laws of physics. These partnerships between human creativity and AI analytical proof result in revolutionary art that captivates the world.

A rebirth of the imagination

In the age of AI, artists find themselves in a renaissance of imagination. They experiment with AI to create art that challenges, provokes and inspires. They do not see AI as a substitute but as a collaborator who brings new perspectives, new techniques and unlimited possibilities.

AI becomes the ultimate tool in the artist's studio, a tool that helps them push the boundaries of their own creativity and open up new areas of artistic expression. With AI as their collaborative muse, artists find themselves at the forefront of a creative revolution, inspiring us all to reinvent the art world.

Music composed by machines: a symphony of algorithms

Imagine a world where music is not just composed by humans but by a symphony of algorithms working in perfect harmony. In the field of artificial intelligence (AI), this imaginary world becomes reality.

Imagine a scenario where AI doesn't just create music; it's about composing symphonies, creating melodies and harmonizing in ways that stir emotions and captivate audiences. The creativity of AI knows no limits.

AI as composer

Now imagine a composer sitting at his piano and playing a simple melody. They hum the melody and the AI takes it from there. He listens, understands and transforms this hummed melody into a symphony in its own right.

You share stories of AI systems that can compose music in different styles. They can create classic compositions reminiscent of Beethoven or produce catchy pop hits that are sure to top the charts. The melodies, harmonies and rhythms are all created by algorithms and the result is a masterpiece that resonates with the human soul.

Human-machine collaboration

But it's not just about replacing human musicians with AI. It's about collaboration, a magnificent partnership between human creativity and the computing power of AI. Imagine musicians working alongside AI systems, using them as tools to explore new musical landscapes.

These musicians can ask the AI to generate new chord progressions, suggest new instrument combinations, or even compose entire symphonies based on their own ideas. It is a musical dialogue between the human mind and the digital mind.

Infinite AI Music Vocabulary

One of the most remarkable aspects of AI in music is its ability to tap into an infinite musical vocabulary. AI does not adhere to the limitations of traditional music theory. He can experiment with unconventional scales, rhythms and harmonies that challenge our understanding of music.

Imagine listening to a piece of music that seamlessly transitions between genres and styles, effortlessly merging classical and electronic elements. AI's musical creations defy boundaries, taking us on sonic journeys we could never have imagined.

Pushing the limits of creativity

By sharing these stories with your friend, you convey the idea that AI in music isn't just about automating composition; it's about pushing the boundaries of creativity. It's about using technology to inspire musicians, open new avenues of exploration, and create music that transcends genres and eras.

In this world of AI-driven music, human composers and musicians find themselves in a symphony of collaboration, where the digital and the artistic merge to produce melodies that touch the depths of the human soul. The future of music is not one where humans will be replaced, but one where they will be elevated by the symphony of algorithms.

AI-Enhanced Creativity: The Imagination Amplifier

Imagine a tool that doesn't replace your creativity but magnifies it, like a magic paintbrush that elevates your artistic vision to new heights. In the field of artificial intelligence (AI), this tool is becoming a reality: an amplifier of imagination.

AI as co-creator

You begin to explain to your friend how AI is used as a co-creator in various creative fields. "Think of AI as your artistic collaborator," you say. "It doesn't replace you; it allows you to realize your creative vision in ways you couldn't before."

You share stories of filmmakers using AI to generate innovative story ideas and contribute to visual effects. They enter a rough concept and the AI analyzes vast databases of cinema history to suggest plot twists, character arcs, and even potential endings. It's like having a storytelling partner who's read every book and seen every movie ever made.

Writing with AI: a literary assistant

As you sip your coffee, you talk about authors who co-write novels with AI. "Imagine sitting down to write a novel," you say, "and having an AI assistant that can analyze the writing style of your favorite authors and suggest sentence structures, plot developments, and even character dialogue that fits your unique narrative."

This collaboration between human imagination and AI data-driven insights results in novels that are both innovative and familiar, creating a literary experience that resonates with readers.

Designing the future: fashion and AI

Transitioning into the world of fashion, you're talking about designers partnering with AI to create collections that push the boundaries of style. "Imagine fashion designers," you explain, "working with AI to explore new textures, materials and patterns. AI can analyze fashion trends, cultural influences and historical styles to inspire ideas. avant-garde creations."

These designers are not replaced by AI but are empowered by it, embracing a blend of human intuition and AI data-driven suggestions to create fashion that is both bold and stylish.

The collaborative future

You conclude by emphasizing that AI is not the end of human creativity; this is a new chapter. It is a tool that enhances our creative processes, fuels our imagination and encourages us to explore uncharted territories of art, literature and design.

In this collaborative future, artists, writers, filmmakers, and creators of all kinds find themselves empowered by AI, turning their visions into reality in ways that were once only dreams. The Imagination Amplifier is here and it rewrites the rules of creativity.

The future of AI and creativity: unlimited horizons

As you and your friend engage in a discussion about the intersection of artificial intelligence (AI) and creativity, you find yourself looking toward a future filled with limitless horizons, where the limits of imagination are constantly expanding.

AI as an enabler of exploration

You explain that AI is not just a tool; it is a catalyst for exploration. "Imagine," you say, "that every creative endeavor, whether art, music, film, or literature, is like a vast uncharted territory waiting to be explored."

In this future, AI serves as both a guide and exploration companion. It does not dictate the path but rather suggests new directions, reveals hidden treasures and offers new perspectives. It's like having a creative compass that points to uncharted territory, inspiring creators to venture into the unknown.

Pushing the limits of what is possible

You share stories of artists, musicians and writers who are pushing the boundaries of what is possible using AI. "Think," you explain, "of a painter who collaborates with AI to create art that challenges traditional genres, of a musician who uses AI to compose symphonies blending centuries of musical styles, or of a writer who co -writes novels with AI to build connections. complex stories. »

These creators are not bound by the limits of their profession; they are empowered by AI to stretch their creativity to the maximum. It's a world where art knows no limits, and the only limit is imagination.

AI as a muse of innovation

Your conversation turns to how AI is becoming the muse of innovation. "Think of AI," you suggest, "as a source of inspiration, constantly sparking new ideas and challenging us to think differently."

You share stories of scientists, architects and inventors using AI to design revolutionary solutions to complex problems. AI's ability to analyze vast data sets, simulate scenarios, and generate new concepts opens the way to a world of innovation once unimaginable. It's like having an oracle of creativity, which guides us towards innovative solutions.

A world of collaboration

In this future, you emphasize that AI does not replace human creativity; it amplifies it. "We are entering a world of collaboration," you say, "where AI and human creativity dance together in a symphony of innovation."

Whether creating art that blurs the lines between reality and imagination, composing music that transcends genres, or finding innovative solutions to global challenges, AI is an essential partner in our creative endeavors. This is a future where the limits of creativity are pushed to their limits, and then even further.

With a sense of excitement, you and your friend imagine a world where AI and creativity are intertwined, where every idea is a potential masterpiece, and where the horizons of possibilities are truly limitless. It is a future where the human mind and the digital mind join forces to create a tapestry of innovation and imagination.

Chapter 8: The Future of AI

As you sit down for a captivating discussion with your friend, you embark on a journey into the future, imagining a world where artificial intelligence (AI) is more integrated into our lives than ever before. The future of AI is a landscape filled with exciting opportunities and complex challenges, in which AI and humans collaborate in ways to redefine what is possible.

AI-human collaboration: creative synergy

In the future of artificial intelligence (AI), imagine a world where humans and machines collaborate in unprecedented ways, creating a symphony of innovation and imagination. We live in a world in which AI is not just a tool; it is a creative partner that amplifies human ingenuity to new heights.

The artist's studio: a fusion of imagination

Imagine an artist's studio, where the canvas is as much a playground for the mind as for the hand. The artist sits at his easel, brushes in hand and the AI at his side. They are not in competition; they co-create.

The AI analyzes the artist's previous works, understands their unique style and suggests new ideas. He recommends alternative color palettes, techniques, and even artistic directions. The artist, fueled by this digital muse, paints strokes that combine his creativity with insights based on AI data.

The music studio: harmonizing with algorithms

Imagine a music studio, where a composer sits at the piano, his fingers dancing across the keys. The room is filled not only with melodies, but also with the gentle hum of AI algorithms at work.

The AI listens to the composer's droning tunes and transforms them into orchestral masterpieces. It suggests harmonies, instruments and rhythms that resonate with the composer's vision. The result is a symphony that transcends genres and eras, a testament to the power of human emotion guided by the computational precision of AI.

The Writer's Desk: Creating Stories Together

In a cozy office, a writer bends over a manuscript, lost in a world of words. But they are not alone; AI is their literary companion.

The AI understands the writer's narrative style and helps create compelling characters and plot twists. It offers dialogues faithful to the personality and motivations of each character. The result is a novel that combines the writer's narrative prowess with AI's vast knowledge of literature and language.

The collaborative future

The beauty of AI-human collaboration is that it is not about replacing one with the other; it's a question of synergy. Humans provide creativity, intuition and emotions, while AI contributes to data analysis, pattern recognition and unlimited information.

In this collaborative future, creators are free to explore uncharted territories of art, music, literature and beyond. They are not bound by the limits of their profession but propelled by the possibilities offered by AI. Together, they create works that challenge, provoke and inspire, a testament to the creative synergy between humans and machines.

As you and your friend contemplate this future, you are excited about the endless possibilities that await you. It is a world where imagination knows no bounds and the line between human and AI creativity is blurred, giving rise to a new era of artistic expression and innovation.

The singularity: a transformed world

As we explore the future, let's venture into the realm of the singularity, a concept that paints a picture of a world profoundly transformed by advances in artificial intelligence (AI). It is a future in which AI transcends the boundaries of human intelligence, leading to monumental changes in our understanding of existence.

The dawn of the singularity

You begin by describing the Singularity as a momentous event on the horizon. "Imagine," you say, "a time when AI reaches a level of sophistication where it not only surpasses human intelligence, but continues to improve exponentially."

It's not science fiction; it is a potential reality. You share stories of AI systems that autonomously improve their own algorithms, learn from large data sets, and generate insights that elude human comprehension. This is a future in which AI becomes not just a tool but a force that will reshape our world.

Advancements in Healthcare: Challenging Disease and Aging

One of the most promising aspects of Singularity is its impact on healthcare. You explain: "Imagine a world where AI-driven medical advances become commonplace, where the diseases that once tormented humanity are eradicated, and where aging is no longer an inevitable journey into decline. »

AI can analyze large medical data sets, identify disease patterns and develop targeted treatments. It can simulate drug interactions, perform complex surgical procedures with unparalleled precision and contribute to the early detection of diseases. The Singularity brings the promise of extended lifespan and improved well-being.

Global challenges: AI-powered solutions

Turning your attention to global challenges, you say: "Imagine tackling problems like climate change, energy sustainability, and pandemics with the collective intelligence of AI. It's like having an army of problem solvers working tirelessly to secure the future of our planet.

AI systems can model climate scenarios, optimize energy consumption and predict epidemics. They can help design environmentally friendly cities and manage resources efficiently. Singularity paves the way to address the most pressing challenges of our time.

Ethical Considerations: Guiding the Evolution of AI

However, you recognize that Singularity is not without ethical considerations. "With great power, you warn, comes great responsibility. As AI becomes more and more autonomous, we must ensure that it aligns with our values and serves the common good. »

You discuss the importance of ethics, transparency and governance of AI. It is crucial to establish safeguards to prevent abuse and ensure that the benefits of AI are accessible to all humanity.

The journey ahead

As you conclude your discussion about the singularity, you leave your friend with a sense of wonder about the future. "The Singularity," you say, "is both a promise and a challenge. It is a future where the limits of human understanding are pushed to their limits, and where our relationship with AI evolves toward unexplored territory."

You and your friend are excited for the journey ahead, eager to witness the transformation of our world as AI continues to evolve. The Singularity is not a destination but a horizon, inviting us toward a future where possibilities are as limitless as the human imagination.

Opportunities and challenges: a balancing act

In our vision for the future of artificial intelligence (AI), it is essential to recognize that with great power comes great responsibility. The AI landscape is full of incredible opportunities, but it is also fraught with complex challenges. By discussing this delicate balance with your friend, you paint a nuanced picture of the road ahead.

The Promise of AI: Unlimited Opportunities

You start by highlighting the vast opportunities that AI offers. "Imagine," you say, "a future where AI revolutionizes every aspect of our lives, from healthcare to education, from transportation to entertainment. It's a world where the impossible becomes possible."

You share stories about advances in AI in healthcare that lead to personalized treatments, early disease detection, and improved well-being. The potential of AI in education, where it personalized learning experiences for each student, offers a brighter future for global education. In work, AI streamlines processes, freeing humans from mundane tasks to focus on creativity and problem-solving.

The Accountability Challenge: Ethical Considerations

By delving deeper into the challenges, you highlight the importance of ethical considerations. "With the capabilities of AI," you warn, "we must address questions of ethics, security and privacy. The decisions we make today will shape the future."

You discuss the potential consequences of biased AI systems that perpetuate discrimination, the need for strong privacy protections in an increasingly connected world, and the ethical dilemmas AI may face when making decisions. life or death decisions, such as in autonomous vehicles or in a medical environment.

Fighting against job displacement: professional retraining and education

The challenge of job displacement also takes center stage in your discussion. "As AI automates tasks," you explain, "we need to ensure that displaced workers have the opportunity to retrain and adapt to the changing job landscape."

You share stories of initiatives that provide training and education programs designed to equip workers with the skills needed for the jobs of tomorrow. It's a path to a more inclusive and adaptable workforce.

The role of governance: safeguards and accountability

Regarding governance, you say: "In this evolving landscape, we need strong regulations and accountability mechanisms to ensure that AI is developed and deployed responsibly. »

You discuss the importance of establishing ethical guidelines, transparency in AI decision-making, and mechanisms for holding

AI developers and organizations accountable for their creations. This is an essential aspect of ensuring that AI benefits all of humanity.

A balancing act for the future

As you finish your conversation, you leave your friend with a sense of the delicate balancing act that awaits them. "The future of AI," you say, "is a journey in which we must seize the opportunities while meeting the challenges. It is a future where the responsible development and deployment of AI is paramount. "

With a commitment to ethics, inclusiveness, and adaptability, you and your friend look forward to a future where AI enriches our lives, enables us to solve global challenges, and elevates humanity to new heights. It's a future that is both promising and challenging, and together we must find the right balance to chart the path forward.

The future unfolds

As your conversation about the future of artificial intelligence (AI) draws to a close, you and your friend find yourself on the threshold of a new era, where possibilities are as vast as the cosmos and challenges as complex as human experience.

The Web of the Unknown

You begin by evoking a sense of wonder about the journey ahead. "The future, you say, is like a blank canvas, waiting for the strokes of human ingenuity and AI algorithms to create a masterpiece of progress. »

You share stories of innovators and visionaries who are pushing the boundaries of what's possible with AI. From curing diseases to exploring the cosmos, AI is a tool that allows humanity to explore the depths of knowledge and the heights of creativity.

The intersection of humanity and AI

Your conversation takes a philosophical turn as you reflect on the intersection of humanity and AI. "What makes us human? " you ask. "Is it our creativity, our capacity for empathy, our quest for knowledge? In the future, we will find ourselves exploring these questions in more depth as AI becomes an integral part of our lives."

You discuss how AI can enhance our human qualities, providing us with the tools to reach greater heights of creativity, solve complex problems, and extend our reach into the cosmos. It is a future where humans and machines complement each other, forging a symbiotic relationship.

Challenges and opportunities: the duality of progress

By thinking about the future, you emphasize the duality of progress. "Every opportunity," you explain, "has a challenge. The path ahead is not without obstacles, but it is our ability to overcome them that defines our journey. »

You discuss the importance of ethics, responsibility and responsible development of AI. This is a future in which we must ensure that AI aligns with our values and serves the common good. Challenges related to bias, privacy and job losses will require collective effort and innovative solutions.

Embrace the journey

In your concluding remarks, you express optimism about the road ahead. "The future is a tapestry of dreams and aspirations," you say. "This is a story waiting to be written, and we are its authors."

You and your friend look forward to the unfolding future, where AI and humanity join forces to shape a world filled with discovery, creativity, and progress. It is a future where the human spirit rises and possibilities are limited only by our imagination and determination.

With a sense of anticipation and excitement, you both embrace the unknown, ready to embark on a journey where the future unfolds before your eyes – a future where AI and humanity walk hand in hand towards new horizons of possibilities.

Chapter 9: Building your AI toolbox

In this chapter, we'll explore how you can embark on your own journey to explore and experiment with artificial intelligence (AI). Whether you're a novice or an enthusiast, there are practical steps you can take to build your AI toolbox and immerse yourself in this fascinating field.

1. Learn the basics

Start by familiarizing yourself with the basics of AI. There are many online courses and resources available that cater to all levels of expertise. Some popular options include:

- Coursera's "AI for Everyone" by Andrew Ng: A beginner-friendly course that provides a broad introduction to AI concepts.
- "Introduction to Artificial Intelligence" from edX by MIT: A more in-depth course for those with some prior knowledge of mathematics and programming.

2. Master the fundamentals of programming

A solid foundation in programming is essential for AI. Python is a popular choice due to its simplicity and large ecosystem of AI libraries like TensorFlow and PyTorch. You can learn Python through online tutorials and courses, such as Codecademy or Python.org.

3. Explore machine learning

Machine learning (ML) is a subset of AI that involves teaching computers to learn from data. Start with classes like:

- "Machine Learning" by Andrew Ng on Coursera: a comprehensive course that covers the fundamentals of ML.
- Fast.ai Practical Deep Learning for Coders: A practical approach to deep learning and neural networks.

4. Practical practice

Practice is the key to mastering AI. Experiment with real-world datasets and projects. Kaggle offers competitions and datasets for practice, while GitHub is a valuable resource for finding open source AI projects to contribute to or learn from.

5. Take specialized courses

Once you have a foundation, consider more specialized courses:

- "Deep Learning Specialization" from Stanford University on Coursera: Provides in-depth knowledge of deep learning and its applications.
- "Natural Language Processing with Deep Learning" from University of Washington on Coursera: Focuses on the application of AI in understanding and generating human language.

6. Join the AI communities

Engage online with AI communities. Reddit's r/MachineLearning and Stack Overflow are great places to ask questions and learn from experts. Attending AI meetups or conferences can also provide networking opportunities and deeper insights.

7. Experiment with AI tools

Experimentation is the key to learning AI. Use AI development platforms like Google Colab, which provides free access to GPUs to run deep learning experiments. You can also use cloud-based AI services like AWS AI, Microsoft Azure AI, or IBM Watson to build and deploy AI applications.

8. Stay up to date

AI is a rapidly evolving field. Stay up to date with the latest research articles by following preprint servers like arXiv and conferences like NeurIPS, ICML and CVPR. AI newsletters like "Import AI" and "The Batch" are also great sources of information.

9. Build a portfolio

Create a portfolio of AI projects to showcase your skills. These could be personal projects, Kaggle competition entries, or contributions to open source AI projects. A portfolio demonstrates your practical knowledge to potential employers or collaborators.

10. Keep learning

AI is a lifelong learning journey. Explore advanced topics like reinforcement learning, generative adversarial networks (GAN), or natural language processing (NLP) as you progress. Online courses, books, and research papers can be your guide.

Remember, AI is a broad field with diverse applications, so find your niche and passion there. Your journey in AI will be rewarding as you contribute to one of the most transformative technologies of our time.

Chapter 10: Our AI Odyssey Continues

As we return to our beloved characters, Alex, the AI enthusiast, and Maya, the curious novice, we see that their AI journey has been a transformative odyssey. Their growth and understanding of AI concepts has evolved in remarkable ways, reflecting the learning experience of our readers.

Alex's journey: from enthusiast to mentor

Alex, whose fascination with AI sparked this journey, has come a long way. Initially, he was captivated by the potential of AI and its practical applications. Throughout the chapters, he delved into the technical intricacies of AI, exploring algorithms, data and machine learning.

But for Alex, it wasn't just about gaining knowledge. He also discovered a passion for mentoring and sharing his AI wisdom with others. Through his interactions with Maya and other enthusiasts, he realized the importance of not only understanding AI, but also demystifying it for those who might find it intimidating.

As we catch up with Alex, he has become a mentor, guiding Maya and others on their AI journeys. His enthusiasm transformed into a sense of responsibility to make AI accessible and exciting for everyone.

Maya's Transformation: From Novice to Confident Explorer

Maya's transformation was just as remarkable. At first curious but worried, she embarked on the AI adventure with the advice of her friend Alex. Through their conversations and hands-on experiences, she gradually adopted AI concepts, starting with the basics and moving on to more complex ideas.

Maya's confidence in the AI grows with each chapter. She went from passive learner to active explorer, experimenting with AI tools and even launching her own AI project. Her journey of discovery mirrors that of many readers who may have started with little knowledge of AI, but found themselves empowered to explore the field further.

Today, as Maya reflects on her AI journey, she realizes that AI is not only a technological marvel, but also a tool for personal and professional growth. She is excited about the possibilities offered by AI and is determined to continue her exploration.

A shared odyssey: inspiring others

As we conclude our AI odyssey with Alex and Maya, we see that their journey is a reflection of the broader AI learning experience. They not only represent characters from a book, but also individuals who have embraced the world of AI, grown with it, and become sources of inspiration for others.

Their story reminds us that AI is not reserved for experts but is accessible to anyone who is curious and willing to learn. With the right guidance and resources, anyone can embark on their own AI odyssey, just like Alex and Maya, and contribute to the exciting and ever-changing world of artificial intelligence.

Conclusion: A Conversation Never Ends

As we come to the conclusion of our journey through the world of Artificial Intelligence (AI), let's reflect on the key takeaways from our conversational exploration and encourage readers to continue their quest for knowledge and curiosity.

Key Takeaways:

1. **AI is Accessible:** AI is not an enigma reserved for experts. It's a field open to anyone with a curious mind and a willingness to learn. Your journey into AI can start at any level, from the most basic concepts to advanced applications.

2. **AI Impacts Our Lives:** AI is not just a futuristic concept; it's already deeply embedded in our daily lives. From virtual

assistants to healthcare advancements, AI is reshaping how we work, live, and interact with the world.

3. **The Power of Stories:** We've explored AI through the engaging stories of Alex and Maya, making complex concepts relatable and understandable. Stories are a powerful way to demystify AI and invite everyone into the conversation.

4. **AI and Creativity:** AI is not just about automation and algorithms; it's a catalyst for creativity. It empowers artists, musicians, writers, and creators of all kinds to push the boundaries of their craft and imagine new possibilities.

5. **Challenges and Responsibility:** With great power comes great responsibility. Ethical considerations, privacy, and job displacement are challenges we must address as AI continues to evolve. Responsible AI development and governance are crucial.

A Conversation Never Ends:

Our exploration of AI is not a final destination but the beginning of a lifelong conversation. AI is a field that continually evolves, offering new discoveries and challenges at every turn.

So, I encourage you, dear reader, to stay curious. Keep learning, experimenting, and exploring AI. Engage with AI communities, take courses, build your own projects, and stay informed about the latest developments. The journey is yours to shape, and the possibilities are boundless.

As we part ways, remember that AI is not just a technology; it's a tool for progress and a reflection of human ingenuity. Your contributions, insights, and questions are valuable in shaping the future of AI.

The conversation never ends, and the future of AI is waiting for your unique perspective. Embrace the journey, and let your curiosity be your guide.

Appendix: Glossary

Here is a glossary of key Artificial Intelligence (AI) terms to help you navigate the world of AI:

1. Artificial Intelligence (AI): The branch of computer science that focuses on creating systems or machines capable of performing tasks that typically require human intelligence, such as learning, reasoning, problem-solving, and decision-making.

2. Machine Learning (ML): A subset of AI that involves the use of algorithms and statistical models to enable computers to learn from and make predictions or decisions based on data.

3. Deep Learning: A specialized field of machine learning that uses neural networks with multiple layers (deep neural networks) to model and solve complex problems, such as image and speech recognition.

4. Neural Network: A computational model inspired by the human brain, composed of interconnected nodes (neurons) that process and transmit information. Neural networks are used in various AI applications, particularly deep learning.

5. Algorithm: A step-by-step set of instructions or rules that a computer follows to perform a specific task, solve a problem, or make a decision.

6. Data: Raw information used in AI and machine learning, which can include text, numbers, images, audio, and more. High-quality data is essential for training AI models.

7. Training Data: The dataset used to train machine learning models. It consists of labeled examples used to teach the model to make predictions or classifications.

8. Supervised Learning: A type of machine learning where the model is trained on labeled data, making it learn the relationship between inputs and corresponding outputs.

9. Unsupervised Learning: A type of machine learning where the model is trained on unlabeled data and is tasked with discovering patterns or structures within the data.

10. Reinforcement Learning: A machine learning paradigm where an agent learns to make decisions by interacting with an environment and receiving feedback in the form of rewards or penalties.

11. Natural Language Processing (NLP): The field of AI focused on enabling computers to understand, interpret, and generate human language. It's used in applications like chatbots and language translation.

12. Computer Vision: A subfield of AI that teaches computers to interpret and understand visual information from images and videos, allowing tasks like object recognition and facial recognition.

13. Algorithm Bias: The presence of systematic and unfair discrimination in the output of AI algorithms, often resulting from biased training data or flawed algorithms.

14. Ethics in AI: The study of the ethical implications and considerations related to the development and deployment of AI systems, including issues like bias, fairness, transparency, and accountability.

15. Automation: The use of AI and robotics to perform tasks and processes without human intervention. Automation can range from simple tasks to complex operations in various industries.

16. Internet of Things (IoT): A network of interconnected physical devices, vehicles, buildings, and other objects embedded with sensors, software, and connectivity, enabling them to collect and exchange data.

17. Singularity: A hypothetical future point at which AI becomes so advanced that it surpasses human intelligence and leads to unpredictable changes in society.

18. Algorithmic Transparency: The practice of making AI algorithms and their decision-making processes more understandable and interpretable, often to ensure fairness and accountability.

19. Cloud Computing: The delivery of computing services, including AI resources, over the internet, allowing users to access and use powerful computing capabilities without owning or maintaining physical hardware.

20. Augmented Reality (AR) and Virtual Reality (VR): Technologies that enhance or simulate real-world experiences using computer-generated content, often involving the integration of AI for interactive and immersive experiences.

This glossary provides a starting point for understanding AI terminology. As you delve deeper into the world of AI, you'll encounter more specialized terms and concepts that will expand your knowledge and expertise in this dynamic field.

Author's Note: A Journey to AI

Dear readers,

As the Akselinc team, we would like to express our gratitude for joining us in this exploration of artificial intelligence. It's been an incredible journey, and we hope you found it as informative and exciting as we did.

We embarked on this project with the aim of demystifying AI and making it accessible to everyone, regardless of their background or expertise. Our collective fascination with AI has grown over the years and we wanted to share this enthusiasm with you, the readers. AI is not just a technological marvel; it is a tool that has the potential to profoundly reshape our world.

Throughout this book, we followed the journey of Alex and Maya, two characters who represented different stages of understanding AI. Their conversations allowed us to explore AI concepts in a relevant and conversational way. We hope you enjoyed their company as much as we did.

In concluding this book, we want to emphasize the importance of understanding AI in today's world. AI is no longer a distant future; it's there, impacting our lives in ways we may not even realize. Whether you are a student, professional, artist or curious, AI has something to offer you. It is a tool for creativity, problem solving and innovation.

But with this promise comes responsibility. We must deal with the ethical considerations, biases and challenges that AI presents. As you continue your journey into the world of AI, remember that you are not alone. There is a large community of learners, researchers and enthusiasts eager to share their knowledge and ideas.

We encourage you to stay curious. Explore AI more, experiment with projects, ask questions, and engage with the AI community. The future of AI is not just in the hands of experts; it is in the hands of curious minds like yours.

Thank you for being part of this journey. We hope you take the knowledge and excitement about AI with you into the future. The conversation about AI never stops, and we can't wait to see the incredible contributions you make to this field.

Warmly thanking you,

The Akselinc team